# Can I do yoga?



Written by Sally Morgan
Illustrated by Emily Hunter-Higgins

Collins

# What's in this book?

Listen and say 1

 Download the audio at www.collins.co.uk/839787

bridge
camel
cat

2 Sam and his mum are in the park.
Sam asks, "What are the people doing?"
Mum says, "They're doing yoga."

Sam asks, "What's yoga? How do you do yoga? Can I do yoga?"

Yoga helps you understand your body. It makes your body strong.

Yoga helps you do your lessons.

Sit on the floor.

Put your hands on your knees.
Close your eyes. Sit and listen.

Stand up. Put your foot on your leg.

Put your arms up. You are a tree.

Be a lion!

Kneel on the floor. Sit back.
Put your hands on the floor.

Open your mouth. Now *roar*!

Be a cat!

Kneel on the floor.
Put your hands on the floor.

Pull up your body, like this!

Be a bridge!

Lie on your back. Put your arms on the floor. Put your knees up.

Push up your body.

Be a snake!

Lie on the floor. Put your hands by your head.

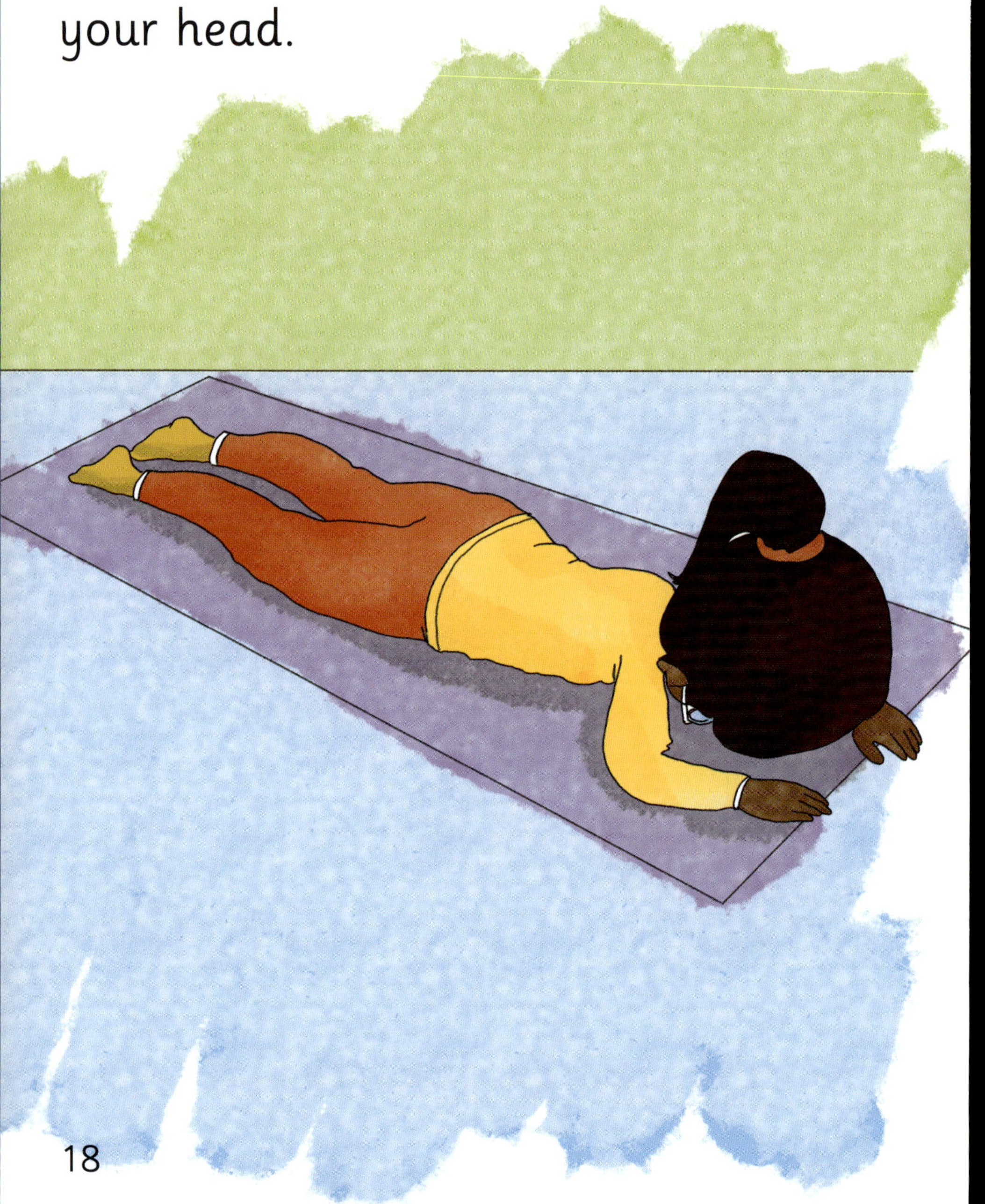

Push up with your arms.

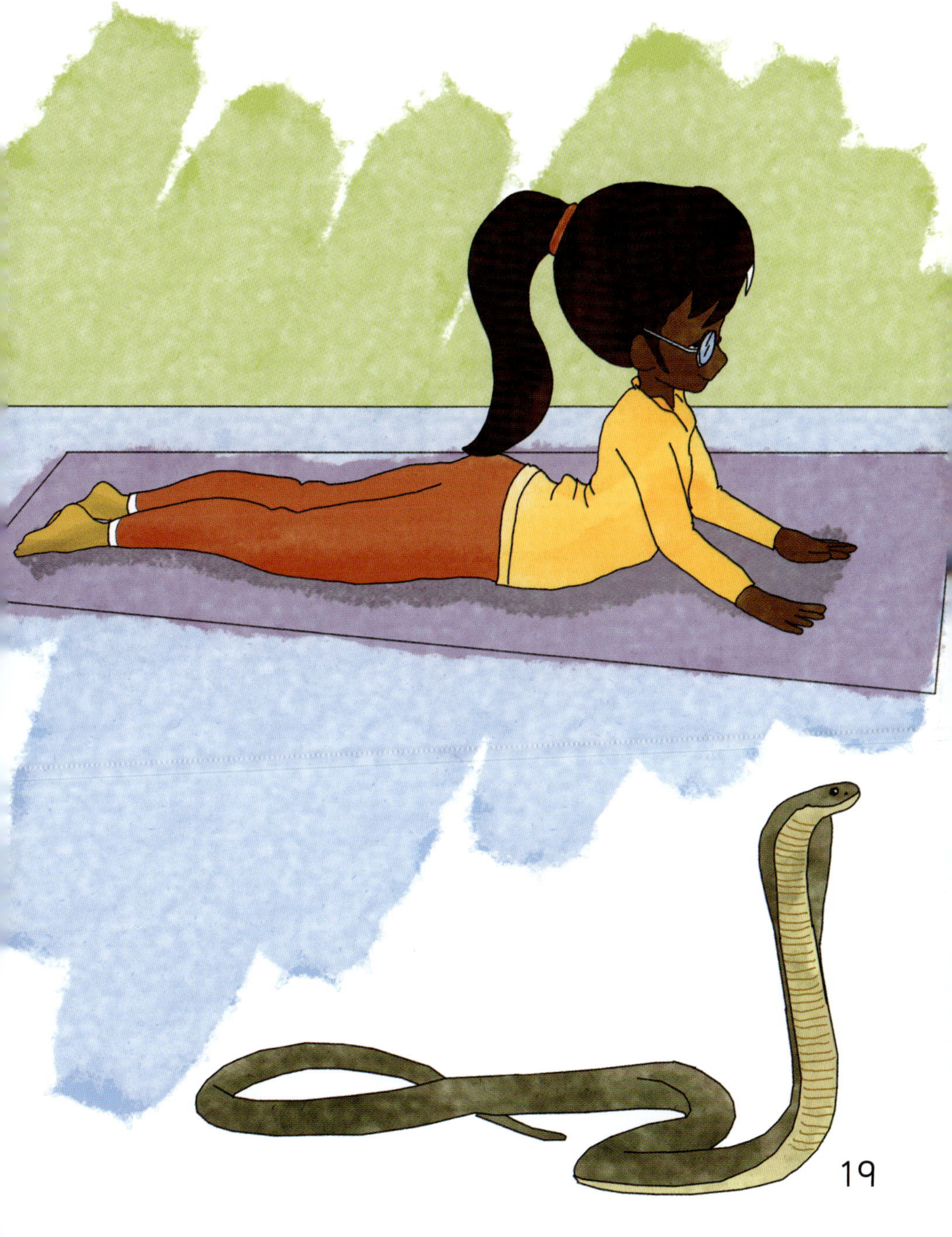

Be a camel!

Kneel on the floor. Put your hands on your back.

Bend back and hold your feet. Look up, and pull!

Now you can do yoga!

# Picture dictionary

Listen and repeat

back

bend

knee

kneel

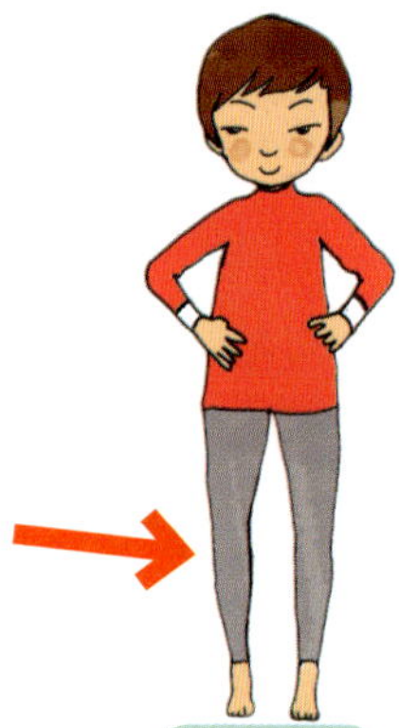

leg

lie

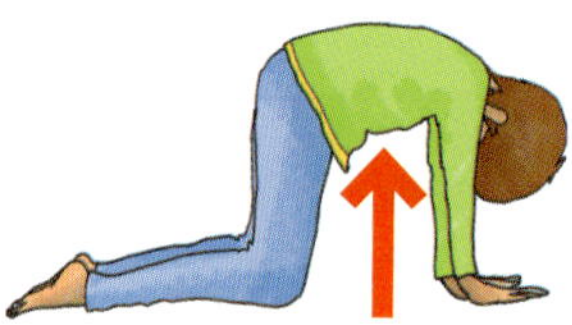

pull up

push up

## 1 Look and match

bridge cat

camel lion

## 2 Listen and say

Download a reading guide for parents and teachers at www.collins.co.uk/839787

# Collins

Published by Collins
An imprint of HarperCollins*Publishers*
Westerhill Road
Bishopbriggs
Glasgow
G64 2QT

William Collins' dream of knowledge for all began with the publication of his first book in 1819.

A self-educated mill worker, he not only enriched millions of lives, but also founded a flourishing publishing house. Today, staying true to this spirit, Collins books are packed with inspiration, innovation and practical expertise. They place you at the centre of a world of possibility and give you exactly what you need to explore it.



10 9 8 7 6 5 4 3 2 1

ISBN 978-0-00-839787-6



www.collins.co.uk/elt



British Library Cataloguing in Publication Data

A catalogue record for this publication is available from the British Library.



Author: Sally Morgan
Illustrator: Emily Hunter-Higgins (Beehive)
Series editor: Rebecca Adlard
Commissioning editor: Zoë Clarke
Publishing manager: Lisa Todd
Product managers: Jennifer Hall and Caroline Green
In-house editor: Alma Puts Keren
Project manager: Emily Hooton
Editor: Barbara MacKay
Proofreaders: Natalie Murray and Michael Lamb
Cover designer: Kevin Robbins
Typesetter: 2Hoots Publishing Services Ltd
Audio produced by id audio, London
Reading guide author: Emma Wilkinson
Production controller: Rachel Weaver
Printed and bound by: GPS Group, Slovenia

FSC
www.fsc.org
MIX
Paper from responsible sources
FSC™ C007454

This book is produced from independently certified FSC™ paper to ensure responsible forest management.

For more information visit: **www.harpercollins.co.uk/green**

Download the audio for this book and a reading guide for parents and teachers at www.collins.co.uk/839787